queer

he

do

N.I.A.

Poems by
Kris Nicholas Conrad

ARCANA
POETRY PRESS

In memory of Judith Dunaway, my first poet friend.

CONTENTS

And if, as the waves compel your clothes
to cling to flesh, you must look away—

Take comfort: Blueprints are never the final
design. The curves and angles that, today,
you want to file down, fill in, invert, erase
will still hold you up tomorrow. Your body
never judges the shape of your mind.

LOVE LETTER TO A NATION

I love the strapping butches
with immaculate manicures,
gravelly whispers,
and hearts of Jell-O
that squish when they wrap you
in their soft strength,
who possessed the secret boyhoods
only a girl can know,
who give you a pet name
like *Dove*,
stride under the rainbow
with swagger and ownership,
and let you sleep
while they drive.

I love the willowy femmes
whose dusky eyes
say *Yes, you*,
who bore their fathers' names
until, shrugging,
they tried on their own,
who carry impossible weight
like they don't even notice
its bearing on their hips,
who throw shade
and punches

with equal expertise,
fearlessly take the top bunk,
and apply Chanel Rouge
Coco Flash
like a goddess
offering the ripest plum.

I love that friend
whose wardrobe is
one-half social worker/
one-half tenured professor,
who wears *that* sweater
and invites you in
from the chill
with a scent
like Saturday evening
in late autumn,
whose throaty chuckles
make you grin, too,
even when you
wear black and blue,
even when you'd thought
you'd run dry.

I love the gentle man
who's outgrown artifice,
who weeps openly

in church and at the movies
because he remembers
the boys whose singalongs
have long gone silent,
who's not ashamed
to ask you to fix his sink,
who moisturizes as if in prayer,
drapes himself
in fine silk robes he can't afford,
and still plays the violin
forty years later,
matches Gloria Gaynor
pitch-perfect
and offers, gently,
to hem your sleeve.

I love the fae folk
who meet your eyes
when they say
How are you today
and really mean it,
who part their hair
with enby/able precision
and invite *Them*
without question,
who park their vegan leather
Doc Martens
carefully by the door

without being asked,
who take off their glasses
when offering reassurance,
whose contentment could make you want
to stop trying
to get whole.

I love the way
you protect your companions
from the rain
and silently step in front
when I'm too scared
to repel the words
that cut us
or repeat the nature
of the crime.
I love the moments
you light cigarettes
for shaky strangers
and offer me shelter
under your smoky jacket.
I love the times
you whisper
You are perfect to me
in my blushing ear,
the way you remind me
It's time to eat,
the way you invite the unready,

warmly, to *Just stay*,
the way cats
clamor for your lap
the moment you
make yourself at home,
the way you are
blanket, garden, hearth fire,
full moon, crowbar,
ever present in breakfasts, memorials,
shirts-on swims,
lights-off confessionals,
twanging acoustic solos,
and the sacred rites
of the orange magic
of queer union.

HEROES ON CASSETTE

Patti Smith's starving
artist neckties
roped me in,
yanked me to the floor,
sat me cross-legged
before the speakers
where I went still, shoulders squared
beneath my black blazer,
my hair crisp
with overzealous gel.
Barefoot on the teal carpet,
I listened, was told
this chesty, guttural rock
is real punk yeah,
but also poetry
(those poems papered
my walls, too, Patti),
and as her rhymes
pressed my chest,
promising Technicolor
in their rocky rhythm,
my best breaths
sent the song
into the strings
of baby butch memory,
hot with *Peace & Noise*,

beginners' night
at the Chelsea Hotel.

Freddie Mercury's supersonic
vocals led me high
through dungeon, low
through opera house,
his sequined catsuit perfect proof
that boys can be glam too.
"Killer Queen" was permission
to sing with my head voice,
just for now with the door
closed, my sashay as fierce
as his "Ay-Oh" echoing
over thousands of heads.
I studied more
about manhood
watching Freddie's flamboyant
swoops, sways,
and bared-chest yodels
flickering above the VH1 logo
than I learned from any
living, chew-spitting
boy-fumbling-toward-man
I ever stood close enough
to smell. His object lessons
in masculine drag—
mustache, leather, dirty Adidas—

felt siblinglike, sensual, protective.
Thanks to Freddie, my skyward-
facing imagination was racing
bicycles into the sugartop
raindrop sky, miles
above hot-pink (Man)hattan
where, down below, dancing
bodies clashed joyously
in the thumping electronic heat
of summer's Friday night.

Tori Amos's piano fingers
birthed (my)r(i)a(d)
concertos atop staff lines
that traced my forming scars.
Her voice never curled
around my name
or quoted my pleas,
but maybe I knew that someday
I would find my own
key to the castle door,
follow her narrative
unwinding up winding stairs
paved with allegory, and
I would spot mermaids
in the bell tower,
waiting for me to announce,
my voice raspy with reason,

"Oh, I understand 'Me
and a Gun' now, Tori,
and you let me inside
this safe house
so I could survive
the sunrise."

Today, those hero hums
are closer than ever;
anywhere I stand,
they purr
crescendos in my ears.
Tori and Patti still breathe
and we will again share air
in the sanctuary of
the crowded concert hall,
but Freddie, to me, has only/
always been a hologram.
His outros were my intro, echoing
ghostlike in distant chambers,
a warning that youth
is not a safeguard
against the hunger
of a virus. I passed
condoms to friends.
Freddie insisted,
his pleas persisting
long after the last time

his fist sliced the hyper-charged air
of an arena,
The show must go on.

My tentative verses
on smudged napkins
and bathroom walls under stuttering bulbs
would have meant nothing
without muse, without courage
in chords that make
me cry hope, croon peace
in the uterus that is my warm bed,
praying in A-flat major
with the silver-haired,
black-jacketed androgyne
intoning rugged verse,
the copper-Venus/faerie goddess
delivering unrepentant soprano,
the coloratura queen strutting
catlike under the moon.

Everyone lives
when they leave behind
song, forever eternal,
for as long as we hit Rewind.

YOUTH STOPPED STILL ONE DAY

In Memory of T.L.V.

You: black-clad blond/blue,
Camel Light menthol
parked between fingers
making points punctuated
by raspy chuckle, heads together
over oversweet coffee.
You praised my poems.
We shared the stage six times
and, countless others,
one of us sat, rapt,
the other blinking
through bright lights
until we found each other's faces
through the backlit dark.

You were tailor-made
for midnights, gritty folk music
thumping the floorboards,
and heartbeat hellos through
each hug. Your gay
was the fearless type,
bold and questing in its approach,
one hand on cocked hip
even if the other sometimes quivered.

Together we teetered
on the edge of adulthood
as if balancing on a rumbling track.
Giggling, we tried on thrifted tomorrows
in yesterday's style,
quaint velvet jackets
too tight in the bust,
a little long
in the sleeve.

Your talent was bottomless
as your speckled ceramic mug on the
insomnia-flecked Denny's tabletop.
(Two creams, five sugars. Always.)
Your joy was hard to read,
disguised as it was in sarcasm,
but always dancing
around your pupils,
bobbing behind
your sensual smirk.
Your smile played. You refused
to act tame. You were
a righteous babe.
I sat in your section
at Cedars Café, and sometimes
you served me. You
always put my coffee down
gently. I never sensed pity

in your bottomless eyes.
You let me be a friend;
you listened with your
whole face.

Your world outlived you.
We lost our onyx charm
May 2001. Death came
by pickup truck,
shoving you aside
like a blackout curtain,
and midnight was over.
At your funeral, all
who had leaned in
to your rainbow
felt lost among the floral sprays
whose color didn't match yours.

If you stepped back on Earth now,
would you even recognize this place?
I've been here all along,
and some days, I barely know
what I'm looking at.

You are only past now;

every girl you kissed is now
a woman in her forties;
your last waking morning
has turned vintage as your clothes.
But while you lived,
you roared.

Your name still echoes in
the Playhouse halls,
and we who loved you,
lion of midnight,
we polish the rusty rails
where you walked unafraid,
and we follow your lead
once more.

TO TELL THE TRUTH (PART 1)

My lies,
painstaking spider webs,
always came close
to touching
the real, the raw.
When I crafted my lies,
I did not paint
over the ugly bumps
of wall that pressed my back:
No razzle-dazzle child's-room blue
or carnival candy pink
obscured the concrete prison
of the dreaded basement.
My lies maintained
the natural, grim,
avocado-night shade
of the truth
that thudded under my feet
like telltale floorboards.

My lies came of age
underground, nurtured
by the smell of leaky pipes,
educated at the famed school
of creaks and cracks.

My lies rearranged the letters
on a Shell station marquee:
PLAY POWERBALL HERE became
HYPERBOLE RAPE WALL, later
PROPEL BEER HALLWAY.
My lies went to sleep
with their eyeliner on.
My lies were glittering clots
of sugary icing
holding together
a crumbling, cakey mess.

Does it matter that I was charmed
before I discovered fear?

Fear chased me
out of my bed,
into the nicotine clouds
in a dimly glowing Waffle House
at the end of time.
The fear summoned my lies
like a fantasy army
of strapping brothers.

The fear pointed at me
and said: *That one.*

I promise: For every story
of mine that was
an eighth, a sliver,
a piddling drop
of a lie,
the author,
my fear,
has always been real,
as real as the sound
of a phone at four a.m.

WATER BALLET
For Kat

You

give me

your arms and your ears and your heart so freely that

I could almost believe you are a starfish, regener

ative and eternal, growing and regrowing,

dancing Tigger-like through the gleeful

sea. Our handfasting will be ribbons

round tubelike wrists. The story

of our love is where *cardio* meets

stoma meets *melō* makes

oikos,   yielding

gent   le *eros*

alw   ays

DREAD NOT (ACROSTIC FOR A GOOD BOY)

Tattered spirit comes clean when
adrift in his blue gaze.
Yawning, he invites me to
lie on the bank of that unending brook,
open my trunk of worries, and
read each one to him.

Dogs crave certainty,
reassurance, the smell of us
eternal and close. His nose on my back
assures me that I can sleep tonight, that
dreams will coast on calm current.
No dog cares if our gender is an earthquake
or questions the motive behind our constant
urge to touch their soft heads. They guide.
Gratitude looks like wet tongue making us giggle,
hair-laden blankets in the wash every Thursday,
tears in our eyes because *he's just so damn cute—*

Animal music is a sacred engagement
calling back those senses we've let grow dull.
Only you, my perfect boy, can get me to
unclench, unwrap my heart, and *howl.* I
sob knowing I can't give you every second,
that sometimes I have to leave you lonely.

If I could know how to convince you that
closing the door between us is never farewell—

I would sleep on canyon floors with you
I would bring you rabbits in my teeth
I promise I promise, yes you are my reason

FOR MY FATHER

Mom Calls You Wild Man

I call you Mild Man.
You're a book, heavy with pages
but always open, like your wisdom
lives in the kitchen, overflowing
with recipes. You speak
with ease. The world
is a Rubik's cube, but
you rotate the rows
with patience.

When Ed Goes to a Party

The guests clamor for my dad
like Jesus on the Mount:
They know—He'll pick up
the dry bread of unfamiliarity,
let his palms crumble the loaf,
and lay down in its place
a feast of friendship,
rich with sauces teeming
with laughter. Dad, your ease
heals scarred hearts. I know:
It's helped mine.

Ed *Is Short for* Educate

Legions grow smarter
just talking to Wild Man.
You stir the pot. Maybe
some people feel safer not knowing.
But you set the current
in motion, and suddenly
the formerly complacent
want to try it, too. So let me
join the wave. You've advised
me to find answers where they nest,
to be unafraid of unknowns.
Every variable gets a name.

Wild Man Fixes Broken Things

Every comfortable seat
contains a secret that, unlocked,
allows the cushions to unfold
into the lushest lounger.
Innovation makes the best things better
and brings back the broken.

Wild Man, you gave me your love
when I felt unlovable,
when I raged
at my own puzzles, when I shoved
their contents to the floor

rather than calmly sorting them
into piles, by color,
edge pieces to the side.

Dad, May I Borrow Your Acceptance?

I see it now. Each puzzle has purpose.
Every decent thing can become better.
Broken does not equal *over*.
The vital tools are curiosity and time.
I hear your insight in my own voice.

Wild Man Had Everyone Fooled

You keep it quiet, an unassuming rectangle
in your back pocket. That puzzler, patience,
when unfolded, opens up
panel after panel like an
endless map, revealing thousands
of interweaving paths to a solution that fits
like a comfortable home. And where
does Ed go when we find the trail's end?
Why, he's back at the door, shoes off,
dinner planned. Give him a call sometime.
He'll pick up.

HANDS DOWN,

As you finger-pick poems,
crafting-shelves-from-rescued-dream
you're building us a home.

You protect me like
firebreaks around the castle;
with night rhymes blacker than lust,

In lust, you play me—
like an instrument of breaths,
my melodies are honey

In love, I write of
kat's-eye moments of your craft;
embracing shadow,

A flicker of you—
lightning, heartbeat, illustrations—
Adoration captured.

YOU'RE SIMPLY MY BEST *for K.*

I write about your
hands. Their power intrigues:
you could crush or create.

you choose to construct—
your hands massage strings, build chords
with echoes that reverberate deep inside.

You stir the pigments
touch lovingly, hold fast, blend,
and paint afterglow.

hands down
you make love that travels light,
landing in the softest center.

Your hands pass me
endless gifts of song and sustenance.
Thank your hands. I do.

SAFE TOGETHER

I'm building a shelter
of cedar bark
and oak leaves.

> *(You can hear the river*
> *You can sleep even*
> *during tornadoes)*

You'll wake
with my heartbeat
on your cheek.
You'll breathe
with fresh air
on your lips

> *(And the sirens*
> *will be a*
> *distant memory)*

We'll remember, together,
to drink water,
to shake out
our shoes and

(The world
will not allow us
to forget)

Ho*(we are,)* w*(ho)*l*(ly).*

HAIKU: IN THE CASITA

In the *casita,*
Ladyfella Corazón
sheds the cool facade,

Tells secrets to Junebug:
loves, pains, powers, her name.
Their bed is a sunrise.

Junebug is cricket,
pilot, wanderer, goddess
but no longer smashed.

Amends like flowers—
these lovers are baking bread
sweet with promises

Like *Today I breathe*
and *Look at the moon, she's full.*
They've survived thus far.

May Junebug press hope
into the earth, nurturing
shoots ready to thrive.

May Corazón keep
a steady pulse and hand, paints
landing where they must.

Two muses made it,
safe, *tejado* holding fast
in the *casita,*

Breathing prayers, yes,
taking calls to meditate,
maintaining love's hearth.

TO TELL THE TRUTH (PART 2)

Every lie I have ever told
was a sick candle
with a half-buried
wick of shame.

I've struck match after match
close to the wax,
nearly illuminating truth,
recoiling with blistered fingers.

Stand closer.
Here is the damage
beneath my skin,
ancient anguish
injected into a baby face
by fear and lying,
low.

The marquee returns a new message,
one *R* forever lost to time:
HEAL. REAPPLY. BE SLOW.

Perhaps my lies
were echoes of my haunted heart,

a sour taste on a
supposedly clean coffee mug.

My lies lie
where I let them fall.
My lies lived long
but I will live longer.

Look, fear led me
by the hand
for so long
I forgot the patterns
of the lines on my own palm.
Fear pushed lies
onto my tongue
until I gagged. Finally, I spit out
those insistent fingers
and my teeth learned to be ready.

Get *fucked*, fear.
My tongue tells truth now.
My throat sings, strong,
confessing
the crimes, the scars
that led my lies and me.

My lips,
dry and quivering,
still form *No*
but now, now
the next word is *More*.

EVEREST AFTER

For Tita and June on Their Wedding Day

Hold fast to the cord
for the entire ascent;
come time for sleep,
take shelter, bodies
close together
in tent
that stays still,
stands guard.

They say most fatalities
occur during descent—
Why? Living is not
an expedition.
Love is not born
at base camp.
Love comes to life
breathing in hitches.
Love is a little, black-eyed
animal whose fur
has grown dense
to preserve heat
at all elevations.

Love is *I'll tell you*
later but I /will/ tell you.

Love is *We'll survive*
descent even
with chilblains
and wind-blindness
because we do
not let go
of the cord.

The key to survival
is:
Find the heart.
Stay close to the heart.
Let its beats be
cadence;
make your rhythm
together.
Keep listening
even when the wind
is demanding
that you go deaf.

On the coldest nights,
backs bent against
the howling,
light gone, bodies
exhausted, say
it together, partake

in the ritual of
staying through:

This cup is warm.
Take hold. Take health.

QUEER HE DOES NEVER IN ANGER

Queer, he does *rage*
when the ballot box
is stuffed with sharks.
Raging, he raises tea,
it will spill before he
lets the West buy his blood.

Never do I *sex*: Two
is not a list, we insist
upon it. Baby I
prayed *boy*, but I played
pink, then I lifted some lip
sticks I wanted to bring.

Man is not a verb. He
adheres to the absurd. He
queerly sees the plot, a plus.
It is not for us. No, *queer*
is for we who are right to rage
but refuse to raise fists in fear.

Love is lift. We can brand
and kiss, but to persist is to
promise: Our anger is for

she who could not live
through the cost, for they
who were lost in the bathroom bust.

Queer means joy born in an
asylum meant to unpray.
Queer pays us after *girl*
means no *man* will be raised.
Queer is our *never* when
rage is our *always*.

We play—we pray—

our way.

ACKNOWLEDGEMENTS

I wish to thank my parents, Ed and Beth Conrad, for their endless support as I have searched for myself and my voice. I also want to thank my partner, Kat Allison, for their contagious creativity, encouragement to write and to share my work with the world, and inexhaustible patience. I would be remiss not to thank Taylor Dog, my four-legged Higher Power, who keeps me laughing and shelters me in his unconditional love. Thank you to my grandparents and uncles, all of whom still walk and talk with me in my dreams. Thank you to my amazing friends, both living and gone, who have read my poems with gusto and, one by one, served as muses. June, Tita, Alyn, Billy, Robert, Christine, Chrissie, Molly, Andrea, Nicholas, Beth, Anneliese, Amelia, Kathleen, Kylie, Dom, Anthony, and so many more — your praise, suggestions, and ongoing reminders that you hear these poems — these are the little pushes that keep me writing. Carina, Taylor V., Ariel, Flo, Bryn, Kasper, Kyle, Shannon, Evan, Sam, Miles, Melissa, Khushi...I miss you greatly and carry you in my heart. There are too many poets to list them all, but thank you, Thomas Sayers Ellis, for sharing your classroom and criticism with me and leaving your mark unapologetically, as you did all things, before you left the world. Thank you, Andrea Gibson, for the light you shared with us to the very end, and thank you, Megan Falley, for being a keeper of that light. Lastly, thank you, Arcana Poetry Press, for bringing this chapbook to life, and thank you, Jordyn Krieg, editor extraordinaire, for your belief in my work, your passion for fine-tuning it into the best it can be, and your endless (and effective!) efforts to bring many beautiful voices together as a powerful illuminant for the reading world.

Kris Nicholas Conrad (he/him) has filled many notebooks, napkins, bound journals, sticky notes, used envelopes, and phone apps with lots and lots of lines, many of which will hopefully never see the light of day. In college, he won the Nemet Scholarship for Excellence in Creative Writing twice. In the present day, Nick is honored to have placed his debut chapbook with Arcana. His poems explore themes of memory, anxiety, community, existing queerly on a quirky planet, healing, recovery, and self-discovery. Nick has published individual poems in several zines and other publications, including the Massachusetts Bards Poetry Anthology 2025, and he reads at poetry events throughout southeastern New England. Nick lives in Eastern Massachusetts with his artist/musician/fix-anything partner and their canine copilot.